"An easy, fun, and riveting read, laced with… some sexy 'sound bites' that will leave you in stitches… literally LOL! The book, penned by a local broadcast legend, gives you a look at the evolution of local news programming and provides historical perspectives on the Civil Rights Movement, race relations, and so much more… A must read!"

Vickie Thomas, WWJ/Entercom Radio
National Association of Black Journalists

"Al Allen was legendary when my career started in Detroit TV. Being from Detroit, I knew of him, but we'd never met. That is, until I got my break in the business as the Fox 2 News Morning traffic reporter in 1998. Al also reported on this show. He gave me the most warm welcome and years of supportive friendship. He was the hardest working, had the most sources, and could turn around more stories in a day than any reporter in town, including the ones half his age and younger. And he did it all without ever looking tired, and always with his smile and endearing laugh at the end of the day. Al Allen taught me so much about the business as a young reporter. He was a great mentor, and for that, I will be forever grateful."

Rhonda Walker
Reporter, WDIV Detroit

"*We're Standing By* is the consummate collection of inside perspectives from the man we saw outside every morning on Fox 2. Al's stories are like written conversations with him — entertaining, insightful, inspirational, and revealing. It's a must-read, and an 'I-can't-put-it-down' for all who have watched, known, and loved Al Allen."

Karen Dumas
CEO, Images & Ideas, Inc.

"Al Allen is a legend, no doubt. He has paved the way for so many in print and broadcast journalism, and is the nicest guy you'll ever meet. This collection of his famed stories and unshared memories of his time in front of the camera are enjoyable, insightful, and a must-read for everyone."

John Mason
Detroit Radio Personality

We're Standing By

Al Allen

Atkins & Greenspan Publishing

Copyrighted Material
We're Standing By
Copyright © 2018 Al Allen
All Rights Reserved

No part of this publication may be reproduced, stored in a retrieval system or transmitted, in any form or by any means — electronic, mechanical, photocopying, recording, or otherwise — without prior written permission from the publisher, except for the inclusion of brief quotations in a review.

For information about this title or to order other books and/or electronic media, contact the publisher:

Atkins & Greenspan Publishing
18530 Mack Avenue, Suite 166
Grosse Pointe Farms, MI 48236

ISBN:
978-1-945875-41-0 (Hardcover)
978-1-945875-42-7 (Paperback)
978-1-945875-43-4 (eBook)

Printed in the United States of America

Cover and Interior design: Van-garde Imagery, Inc.

Cover photo: Richard Roethler
Photograph courtesy of station WJBK.

Photographs used with permission. All uncredited photographs courtesy of Al Allen's personal collection.

Dedication

We're Standing By. Dedicated to the best grandsons a family can have, Andrew III and Evan, along with the rest of the family.

Wife, Alfreda, son, Andrew Jr., and daughter-in-law, Yolanda.

Can't forget the lady who would call the station and say, "Tell that boy to put a hat on his head," or "Tell him he's too close to the street!" — my mama.

My grandsons, Andrew III and Evan.

Acknowledgements

It was not my looks, voice, or writing skills that made me who I am today.

It was a team that helped open the door. Can't name everyone, but you know who you are.

Thanks for your blessings, support, and advice.

One in particular: Kathy Young Welch.

Kathy was my assistant news director at WJLB-FM 98. I had some crazy ideas, and Kathy helped make those crazy ideas come to reality.

Contents

Dedication v

Acknowledgements vii

Foreword xi

Introduction xiii

Chapter 1	Overworked and Underpaid	1
Chapter 2	Mis-cue	5
Chapter 3	Second Time's a Charm	9
Chapter 4	Showed Up and Showed Out	15
Chapter 5	Eighteen with a Bullet	19
Chapter 6	"We're Standing By"	23
Chapter 7	Proud to be Funky	27
Chapter 8	Livernois Riot	31
Chapter 9	You Own the Story... "Breaking News"	37
Chapter 10	Right Place at the Wrong Time	41
Chapter 11	Are Television Newsrooms Black and White?	43
Chapter 12	Never Kiss and Tell	47
Chapter 13	So, You Want to Be a Journalist?	51

Chapter 14	Who is Al Allen?	53
Chapter 15	Is it Real or Fake News?	59
Chapter 16	Colder than a Well Digger's Ass in Montana	61
Chapter 17	Open the Door — Let Me In	65
Chapter 18	Bad News in the Big City	69
	Biography	75

Foreword

IN AN AGE IN which the White House tries to declare that facts are fake, and that the truth is a lie, those who serve on the front lines of history deserve special praise and attention.

Al Allen deserves every award and accolade he's received in his 50-year career. He is one of Detroit's greatest heroes, the iconic reporter who witnessed some of the region's most important events and always told us the "Truth!" about what happened and why.

Sometimes, the truth was difficult to watch.

"Crime by Color" — Al's ground-breaking documentary regarding black-on-black crime in Detroit — forced us all to examine the causes of the violence on our neighborhoods. He was right there on the corner, dodging bricks, bottles, and Molotov cocktails, when an angry crowd confronted police in the summer of 1975.

He was right across the street when an irate client walked into a Detroit law firm and started shooting, killing the secretary and wounding an attorney.

He was right there on the scene for plant closings, layoffs, school shutdowns, and strikes.

But, Al Allen was also the calm and reassuring voice that helped us all start our day and get out the door. Through every blizzard and every storm, Al was always "Standing by!" He was ready to "Go live!"

"We're Standing By"

He was a traffic cop, forecaster, and preacher rolled into one, reporting on the obstacles ahead, and telling us how to get around them. No matter what the story or the circumstance, he always found the right words to guide us home and lift our spirits.

As Al retraces his personal and professional life in this autobiography, you may find yourself remembering some of the history-making stories he covered. You may also find yourself remembering why Al (aka Andrew Long) Allen became such a beloved reporter at Fox 2.

Without him, the mornings are colder, the clouds are thicker, and the storms are more frightening. We miss him every day. But it's good to know that his wit and wisdom can always be found in the pages of this book. Enjoy!

Huel Perkins, Anchor
Fox 2 News Detroit

Not only was Fox 2 News Anchor Huel Perkins my trusted colleague, he became my good friend.

Introduction

IF I WERE DOING a TV news report about my journalism career, I would compare it to a snowball rolling down a hill. It just kept getting bigger and bigger, until it became an avalanche.

I'm about to tell you all about it in my autobiography, *We're Standing By*. I even wrote this book in the style of TV newswriting, using very short sentences and a lot of ellipses, which simply mean *pause between the words*. This is not the traditional way of writing a memoir, but it's the way Al Allen tells stories, including his own stories.

So, put on your seatbelt for one hell of a ride.

In TV news, you see or hear the finished product in front of the camera or behind the microphone. But in this book, I take you on a background journey that began nearly half a century ago. I guess you can say, I was at the right place at the wrong time.

We're Standing By is meant to inspire, educate, inform, and entertain. Not as long as the Bible, but the message may be just as powerful. Well, just a thought.

No matter the weather, the chaos and confusion… We're standing by… Al Allen reporting.

Chapter 1

Overworked and Underpaid

APRIL 1995. WORKED FOR Channel 2 for 11 years.

Still running like I stole something. My agent keeps reminding me that my audience recognition tops any on-air talent in the market.

My reaction: Just doing my job.

Actually, contract negotiations started six months early. My contract was due to expire in October. Well, I found out from someone close to corporate accounting — I can't name the person — I was making pennies while others were making dollars. Throughout my career, my work spoke for me. The bottom line: Fox 2 was offering a one to two percent salary increase. That's like being kicked in the desert with no water.

The countdown was on, that's why we started negotiations a half year early. May and June came and went, talks went like cement, stuck at one to two percent. Quietly and unnoticed, I began cleaning out my locker.

In July, I fired my agent. Obtained the services of a new agent. He was talking, but management appeared not to be listening. My story output was three to four stories a day, while some reporters were averaging one or two stories every three months. It appeared to me that some of the reporters had more aggressive agents.

Mine, well, all talk and no action. Near the end of August, getting close to crunch time, the clock ticking... I felt betrayed, misused, and abused. I kept all this in. Finally, I hired a third agent. They say three strikes and you are out. Marc Whitfield is a labor lawyer; some of his clients included veteran anchor Carmen Harlan at Channel 4, Detroit's NBC affiliate, and several anchors and reporters at Channel 2. Well, Marc is a no-nonsense attorney and by the middle of September, he worked out a 12 percent pay raise, along with a few other fringe benefits. I got in this mess myself, and I didn't expect drama like a six o'clock news story...

Looking back, getting to this point was sometimes rocky... Hit a few detours and bumps in the road, but in the end, rewarding. Had it not been for a few friends opening the door, my success could have been just a dream. My grandfather always said, "Always be on your best behavior, because you never know who's watching."

Sound Bites

Often asked: Who were some of the most influential people you've interviewed? Well, you cannot leave out US Federal Court of Appeals Judge Damon Keith. This district includes Michigan, Ohio, Kentucky, and Tennessee, and is known as the Sixth Circuit. Keith, myself, and a few other journalists were being honored by Wayne State University's School of Journalism. Sitting next to each other, our conversation ranged from civil rights, education, social issues, and the state of African Americans. Judge Keith's decisions have affected many high-profile cases, both locally and nationally. Judge Keith is also known as a warrior for civil rights.

Back in 1980, Ronald Reagan had just won the Republican Party presidential nomination at the Republican National Convention held in Detroit. I made friends with a black Secret Service agent. Asked him a favor: "Where can I stand when Reagan comes out, so I can try and get a quick interview?"

The agent told me where.

As Reagan walked by, I stuck my microphone out and got the interview, thanks to the African American agent.

As City Hall reporters, Burt Allen (no relation) and yours truly ran the bureau like jockeys riding thoroughbred horses. Decided to throw a Christmas party, which included a lot of holiday spirit. Even invited Mayor Coleman Young. Knew he was going to be a no-show.

Well, to our surprise, the Mayor showed up, but the booze was gone. He cussed us out, called us "You MFs," but then invited us to his office for a few drinks and conversation. Oh, what a night.

Chapter 2

Mis-cue

BACK IN THE EARLY 1970s, I landed at WJLB-AM radio, following nearly two years at WGPR-FM as an anchor/reporter/board operator.

WJLB represented a big career change, so I thought. I was hired as anchor/reporter. It was a learning experience. However, my work had not gone unnoticed. The news director at WCAR, the second all-news radio station, apparently had been listening, and after nearly two years at WJLB, I was offered the position of City Bureau Chief and Weekend Anchor.

Say no more… I took the job. The bureau office was around the corner from the mayor's office, the eleventh floor of City Hall. I joined the staff, which included both local Detroit newspapers and a couple of other radio stations. One was CKLW, the Windsor, Canada, station. That's when I met Burt Allen. We became partners in crime covering metro Detroit news like a cheap suit. We did this by:

A. Developing sources;

B. Getting exclusive tips from politicians to police;

C. Exposing those hiding in closets;

D. Mentoring young journalists like Vickie Thomas and Pat Sweeting; and

E. Winning journalism awards from the Associated Press and United Press International for Best Documentary, "The Murder of Otto Wendell," best friend of union boss Jimmy Hoffa, who disappeared several months before Wendell was killed.

After a couple of years at WCAR, I found myself unemployed. The station was sold to the singing cowboy Gene Autry, and the format changed to country-western music. This was a miscue, a term we use in TV news when someone airs the wrong video. No Plan B. I had a wife, a son, and a mortgage. So what do I do?

- By night, I became a DJ at the Old Argyle Night Club, spinning records; and

- By day, I worked as a loan officer at a downtown loan office.

Spinning records, I became friends with John Hudson, a record promoter. Found out we were both from Little Rock, Arkansas. Asked if he could help find me a job back in radio. After a few months, he told me he'd had a conversation with WJLB Program Director Jay Butler, and Butler was looking to fill a position in the news department. I called Jay, and went down to make an audition tape. A few days later, I was hired.

"Whew!" I had been at the end of the road, stranded, when finally this opportunity put me on a new path back into journalism.

At the time, the WJLB news department was what is called "rip and read." That means *rip* the news report off the news wire (the machine that prints stories coming from the Associated Press and United Press International) and simply *read* it on the air.

My plan: make it "rip and rewrite," and go out and cover stories. My vision: establish an award-winning, multi-news staff that's well-respected in the community. Can you do this on a soul music radio station?

Sound Bites

Take out a stopwatch… At Fox 2, the average length of a story was 1:40 — one minute, 40 seconds. Carla Gaines, producer and supervisor, kept cutting down story time to finally around a minute, and that includes interviews (sound bites), video, reporter on camera, and the close. This left a lot of reporters grumbling. They told me, "You come from radio news — you can do it." Well, we actually did a complete story, which we called a "package," in under 25 seconds. Can't believe it included interviews, video, and an on-camera close. Can anyone beat that?

What's in a name? Well, reporter Nikki Grandberry always called me "Gramps," even though I was in my 30s. Asked Nikki why. Said I could keep secrets, especially when colleagues told me confidential information about themselves. Yes, just call me Gramps.

I told you about sources… Well, here's a tip for you, and you didn't hear it from me. Trying to locate the mayor, governor, county executive, and so on? Don't ask their press person; instead, make friends with the scheduler. That's the person who makes out the daily schedule for the person you are looking for. Thanks!

Chapter 3

Second Time's a Charm

THEY SAY THE THIRD time's the charm, but that was true for my second stint at WJLB, and the newsroom needed a news hit. My boss, Jim Reese, the news director... Smart, nice, and a grammar guru. Jim spent more time outside of the newsroom working as a model for major retailers.

As a result, the news department lacked leadership and direction. That's when I decided to step up to the microphone with a plan. Presented it to the general manager, Norman Miller, and sales manager, Commodore Clark. They liked it.

First, Jim Reese was out, and I was in as the news director. An unhappy Jim Reese let me know he felt I set him up to fail. Well, I was excited that doing things my way and having the courage to take the lead resulted in a promotion. My plan was to:

A. Expand the news staff;

B. Increase the number of newscasts;

C. Sell advertising on newscasts at a higher rate;

D. Replace rip-and-read with rewriting wire stories and add coverage for news stories;

E. Create an entertainment segment, something that had never been done before.

Advertisers and listeners loved the change — music and information together.

In the late 1970s, WJLB made the big switch from AM to FM, and moved to a new downtown location from the Broderick Tower to the Penobscot Building. Following the move, I increased the news department from three to seven people over time.

Finally, we became a major news player in town. Keep in mind, we were a black-programmed music station. However, I still had my eye on the prize: becoming a television news reporter/anchor. I applied and was denied at all three local stations. The main reason? Lack of TV experience.

But Phil Nye, Channel 7 news director, gave me hope, advising, "Don't leave the market, watch the newscasts, and learn television techniques."

Meanwhile, WJLB hired a new general manager, Verna Green. She gave us the green light to explore more news information options. One was a live, phone-in talk show, which we called "Talkback," covering everything from politics, grassroots organizations, crime, social issues, and more.

Just like a sports playbook, the WJLB newsroom had its own playbook. This time, I encouraged the news staff to produce special reports and documentaries.

My first was about alcoholism in the black community called "Merry Go Round of Denial, the Black Alcoholic." The next, "Crime by Color," explored black-on-black crime.

Both were meant to be a wake-up call in Detroit's black community. They won a truckload of national and local journalism awards around the country, including The Robert F. Kennedy Awards for Excellence in Journalism, making WJLB the first black radio station in the country to win this top journalism award.

In addition to news, we were winners in sports reporting with Herman McKalpain's "Inside the NBA." Jim McFarlin, entertainment reporter for *The Detroit News,* spotlighted his "Big Mac" award. We were consistent winners in broadcast news.

All that gold started to tarnish with the hiring of a new program director, James Alexander. He was known for answering the phone by saying, "James A., 24 hours a day."

Looking over the numbers, our news department was more popular than music programming. James Alexander warned me that this would have to change. Alexander — who stood about six feet, five inches tall, was a heavyweight, and seemed to sweat constantly, even in the winter — began to dismantle the news department, cutting the news staff and newscasts.

But not without a fight. I'm a short guy, and sometimes the Napoleon complex would come out of me. Our conversations were often confrontational and loud with a lot of finger pointing. Well, we were the talk of the station.

Air personality the Electrifying Mojo pulled my coat tail, warning that James was going after my head. In the Bible, David whipped Goliath's ass. In my case, Alexander was my boss. All I could do was start looking for another job.

Fortunately, God has a way of turning a bad situation into a good one. Bill Vance, news director of WJBK-TV, had been reading about our award-winning news department. He offered me a position on the assignment desk. However, I wanted to be in front of the camera. We met and discussed my future at WJBK-TV. What could I do to convince Vance that I was ready to make the transition?

"Find a real story," Vance told me. "One that could be air-able."

I did just that with Furman Barnes as my shooter. Shooter is what we called our camera operators. We did the story, complete with an on-camera stand-up, which means standing in front of the camera and doing a live report. Furman helped me put the story together.

A few weeks later, Bill Vance called and offered me the job as anchor-reporter. Of course, I accepted. TV reporter meant a bigger audience, and of course, more money... So I thought.

"Al, show them what you can do first," suggested close friend and advisor, Attorney Elliott Hall. Leaving WJLB, I was making $33,000 a year. WJBK offered me a $2,000 increase. Of course, I expected more, but accepted what was offered.

Sound Bites

No, she didn't...

Covering the opening of the new MGM Grand Casino, a woman walks up wearing a long coat. Said she had been lying in bed naked, watching me covering the grand opening of the MGM, so she decided to come and see. Opened her coat. (Oh, no!) She was wearing clothes...

Dangerous job?

Standing in line at the bank. All of a sudden, I felt a sharp pain in my arm. Turned around, a lady had pinched me, she said, to make sure I was real.

Another dangerous job...

Interviewed Butch Jones, cofounder of Young Boys Incorporated, a notorious and violent Detroit drug ring. Just released from prison, Jones had written a book about YBI. Did the interview in a rundown house, surrounded by gun-toting security. What would have happened if... *Whew!*

The Hitman makes a big hit on WJLB radio... While anchoring the news, WJLB commentator Jim Ingram stopped by and asked me to interview a young, up-and-coming boxer, who was turning pro that weekend. His name: Thomas "Hit Man" Hearns. I interviewed Hearns. Sure enough, he knocked out his opponent, thus becoming one of the greatest fighters in boxing history.

Not blocking my shot...

I have a bad habit of physically blocking someone who refuses to do an interview. Only this time, it was Detroit Pistons player Rick Mahorn. Six feet, five inches, weighing nearly 250 pounds... I came up to his knees. He couldn't move, and I got the interview. Ask my shooter Mike Shore...

Chapter 4

Showed Up and Showed Out

AH YES... IT WAS my turn to burn.

I hit the ground running. Like I stole something. Had a lot to prove in a short period of time. Second day on the job, I did my first live shot. Felt like a veteran. Initially, management wanted to wait a week until I felt comfortable. Not Al Allen. I was hotter than the Fourth of July. In fact, I:

1. Began anchoring the morning newsbreaks;
2. Served as the live host for the United Negro College Fund Telethon;
3. Worked as the live host for the Jerry Lewis Telethon;
4. Hosted a weekly public affairs show;
5. Served on the Board of the National Academy of Television Arts and Science (local Emmy Chapter); and
6. Did all this while reporting.

Can I catch my breath? (*Whew!*) Hell no...

"We're Standing By"

My mentor was Joe Weaver, Channel 2 auto reporter. His philosophy:

1. Have a liquid lunch;

2. Pay for your photographer's lunch; and

3. Make sure you're on camera a lot when it's time to renew your contract so management knows who you are.

A few months on the job, ran into General Manager Bill Flynn. Welcomed me to Channel 2, then told me how well his wife liked me on the air. Well, I guess my job was secure.

Running late to a news conference, my shooter, John Dumontel, wanted to light up the room. Had his big light kit, which included lights, light stands, and cords. Told John we really didn't have time. He responded, "A, watch." Less than two minutes… the lights were up, and the room looked like a picture. Made it just in time. (Wow.)

Quick lesson: unlike radio where you work alone, in television news, you're part of a team.

In television news, you live and die by the clock. Deadline pressure makes the air so tense, you can cut it with a knife. In the newsroom, this creates a daily agenda that includes shouting, cussing, kicking trash cans, and throwing typewriters in the air (this, of course, before digital), usually aimed at someone. When the smoke settles, it's showtime.

With my radio news background, the transition to TV news was very smooth. Those television techniques? I learned what they meant.

Being a news veteran, the Detroit market may be the best in the country. From crime, business, education, and social issues, Detroit offers it all right here, right now. The hours can be long, but the finished product is priceless. Journalism is often referred to as the Fifth Estate, meaning the right to report the news. However, I've always considered it a privilege.

Sound Bites

Growing up in the segregated South as an African American, you knew your place: separate, not equal.

Movie theatres: whites on the main floor, blacks the balcony. One Saturday, I went to "Annie Oakley," a weekly TV show about a cowgirl. This particular Saturday, there was a drawing for a gift. My number was called. Started to run downstairs to get my gift. Stopped. Said to myself, "This floor is only for the white section." Thought about it again. Ran downstairs and got my gift. No one stopped me. So much for segregation.

Just trying to be creative for a date in high school… Had a job and a car – a 1953 Mercury ragtop convertible. Went to Motown Records to buy records. The warehouse was in the basement. Had an idea. Asked the secretary, could I bring a date and sit in the lobby and possibly meet some of the Motown talent as they came in? Thanks to the secretary, it worked. Would say hello to Marvin Gaye, Smokey Robinson, and they would respond. My date, she was mine, and you could sing a long list of Motown songs to describe all the fun we had.

Then a music mishap… Popular morning show DJ at WJLB was the late Al "Perk" Perkins. He was bringing an R&B concert to the Fox Theatre. The late Natalie Cole was headlining the show. The day before, Cole arrived at Detroit Metro Airport, where she was busted for carrying cocaine. Perkins would have to put up $10,000 cash to get her out in order to perform. Perk phoned me, calling Cole all kinds of vulgar names, gave me a check for ten grand, went to the airport, and picked up Natalie Cole. The concert? Didn't miss a beat. Al Perkins was hotter than the Fourth of July. Never again.

Chapter 5

Eighteen with a Bullet

"Eighteen with a bullet" — that's radio music terminology. It means a newly released record is headed to number one, faster than a speeding bullet.

Over the years, trying to put together a Channel 2 morning show was like trying to climb Mount Everest wearing ice skates. Affiliated with CBS, we provided five-minute local newsbreaks during the national morning news program. Attempts were made to expand the local newscast. Initially, Joe Weaver and Nancy McCauley anchored; I reported outside. In a few weeks, due to overtime, it was cancelled.

Then in 1992, we struck a groove. An all-local newscast was launched, and it took off like a rocket. Around that same time, we became an "O&O" (owned and operated) station for the Fox Network. Unlike the local competition, which dumped to the network at 7:00 a.m., we continued with local news until 9:00 a.m.

The concept? Viewers in the morning were not sitting and watching Fox 2, but they could hear us while getting the kids ready for school and preparing for work. It was local news: all the news, all the time. Ratings shot through the roof. From nowhere... to number one. Alan Lee and Lucy Noland anchored, with Kam Carman doing weather, Rhonda Walker on traffic, and, of course, Al Allen, live every half hour on the streets.

As the young kids say today, the newscast was "dope." Someone was thinking ahead: we used two live trucks in case one broke down. The morning news show was redefined, rediscovered, and reenergized. We were on fire, burning up the airwaves with our popularity spreading like wildfire.

Unfortunately, we were airing video of fire, plane crashes, and crumbling skyscrapers, with the United States under attack, the beginning of 9/11. We had just pulled into a restaurant parking lot – Doug Tracy, Greg Tatchio, and me – when we were ordered to head to Metro Airport ASAP. The objective? Interview passengers coming in from New York City. We were there until around four o'clock. We did dozens of live shots for our local station and live shots for the Fox affiliates around the country.

Afterward, we felt like we had been beaten up and kicked to the curb. This was the first true test of the morning show, and we kicked ass.

Sound Bites

I gave you fair warning. On the weekends, I ran the sound board for Reverend Robert Grant's gospel show on WGPR-FM radio. Reverend Grant would say, "I feel the Holy Ghost!" Then he'd run out of the studio, up the stairs, and out the door. Well, I warned him: "Run out the door again, and you will be locked out."

He ran out, and I locked him out...

Where's the door key? Photographer was outside the live truck, setting up. With the engine running, I jumped out, and somehow hit the lock button. We were locked out, had to wait outside in the bitter cold for nearly an hour for someone to bring us a key.

Speaking of live trucks… They are often called "caskets on wheels." When you raise the mast (which transmits the signal back to the station), it's about four stories tall and can attract lightning during a thunderstorm. The equipment can become electrified if the mast is hit by lightning, causing death or injury to anyone in the truck. This has happened. Today, during a lightning storm, the mast has to be lowered…

We're covering a school shooting, interviewing Chief Ike McKinnon, who's surrounded by other reporters. I misspoke the chief's name by saying, "Thank you, Chief Hart." Well, Chief Hart was in prison for corruption charges. (Oops!)

Chapter 6

"We're Standing By"

I repeated those words about every half hour, just before a live shot. To the producer, director, and audio person, it was a cue that we were ready to go live. Sometimes we would hit a live shot with just seconds to spare. We did so many different live shots, at so many locations, sometimes I would forget where we were. Detroit, St. Clair Shores, someplace else? How can we be at one location and less than 30 minutes later at a second location? Seems almost impossible.

Yes, we broke many speed limits, but we had a new tool. We were the first in the market to use "Look Lives." That's a report that looked live, but was actually pre-recorded to give us time to get to the next location. Sometimes we had to do two Look Lives, like if we were downtown Detroit and had to be live on the University of Michigan campus in Ann Arbor, which was at least a 45-minute drive away.

With a radio background and lots of ad-lib experience, everything had to be right the first time; no two or three takes allowed. Of all the stories I've done, live and on tape, viewers most remember me standing on overpasses in snowstorms or heavy rainstorms as we — my two-person crew and myself — battled Mother Nature's sucker punches, sometimes with ten-below-zero temperatures or torrential rains drenching us in a matter of minutes.

No matter the weather, we weathered the elements. Just like the mail carrier, live news must go on. Besides weather, there were building fires, multi-vehicle accidents on the freeways — all live, all the time. One casualty of working outside was spending money buying new suits, shirts, ties, and shoes, because Mother Nature took her toll on my attire.

Working the morning shift, you would think the workload could be overwhelming, but here I go with other ideas, increased speaking engagements, and public appearances. I even dabbled in the music business, considering that a source of future retirement income. Ever since working in radio, I was invited to speak at churches, community events, and schools, and I was often asked to serve as master of ceremonies. The list read like a restaurant menu. My vision for public speaking was to raise the roof and get the audience swept up in the moment.

They say practice makes perfect. The more you speak, the better your presentation and delivery. Dr. Martin Luther King's *I Have a Dream* speech — which was actually less than 10 minutes long — lasted nearly an hour. That means that notes and ad-libs comprised the rest of it.

Speaking off the top of your head? How about that. Radio personality John Mason and I were coworkers at WJLB. He introduced me to Karen Dumas. Karen worked in radio as a talk show host. She was a publicist, involved in public relations. I met her husband, Tim, and the couple's two children. Karen is well connected with the movers and shakers in Detroit.

Our friendship led to more paid speaking engagements. We were a hit. Just a coincidence, Fox 2 Anchor Huel Perkins and I teamed up to become the double-dose of speaking engagements. If Huel couldn't make an engagement, I would step in for him, and vice versa. I developed the delivery and cadence of a Baptist preacher, which at times had the sisters running down the aisles.

I ain't done yet... Music was my other love. I developed friendships with entertainers, record executives, and producers. Like Invictus records, Brian Spears, superstar producer, Mike Powell (Anita Baker and others), and record producer Mike Stokes, known as the hit maker. With their help and advice, I started A-2 Productions and a music publishing company, Kick Booty Publishing. Formed and managed a seven-piece funk and soul band called Yo Daddy's Band. Played cover songs in Vegas, off the strip. Hired a road manager named Tiny. The band made some money. After a couple of years, my music venture hit a sour note. I lost my love and left the music business. Had to take care of Uncle, moving him from Phoenix, Arizona to Southfield, Michigan. He was suffering from Alzheimer's.

Sound Bites

Call this… reporter involvement. Along with other reporters, spent the night outside in the bitter cold, around 15 degrees, to dramatize the plight of the homeless sleeping outside in frigid temperatures.

No, he didn't... Beginning of his second term, Mayor Coleman Young rolled out this huge multi-million-dollar development project. After several months, I pulled the mayor aside, asked him what happened to the project? The mayor's response: "I lied." What a hell of an exclusive story!

Speaking of Mayor Young... Burt Allen and I were standing, covering a story at Cobo Center. Sitting in the stands behind us: Mayor Coleman Young and Federal Judge Damon Keith. All of a sudden, we heard a loud thud. Then a big champagne bottle rolled out from the stands. We looked up; the mayor looked down. Told us, "Don't say a damned thing."

Chapter 7

Proud to be Funky

James Brown, the Godfather.
I've interviewed a lot of entertainers over the years: movie stars, singers, and entertainers. To me they were not special... not celebrities... just people. But one stands out.

James Brown, the Godfather, Soul Brother Number One, and the hardest working man in show business. Attending a James Brown concert leaves you tired and worn out. You are going to shout and dance. Spellbound and speechless. The energy level hits a 15. His musical groove... yes... funky...

As a performer, he was engaging. I once served as master of ceremonies at an R&B concert at the Robinson Auditorium in Little Rock, Arkansas. Introduced James Brown and the Famous Flames...

Years later, rode in a limo with Brown. Went to see Reverend C. L. Franklin, father of Aretha Franklin, who was in a coma at Henry Ford Hospital in Detroit at the time. Talked about music, social issues in the black community, and politics. Later that night, took the family to a James Brown concert. Had front row seats.

The next day, I interviewed James Brown for an entertainment segment. Brown talked about his fight with the FCC — the Federal

Communications Commission, the watchdog of the broadcast media. In one of his songs, he used the word "funky" — the FCC described it as vulgar and indecent.

After a few months, the ban was lifted. Making hit records so fast, many black-owned stations refused to play them. Brown began buying radio stations across the country so his records would be played. Unlike other entertainers, James Brown recorded all his songs live in the studio, just like his live concerts. Brown told me he wanted that same feeling in the studio. And just like Ray Charles, Brown kept all of his masters...

Sound Bites

After 9/11, security was tighter than someone wearing a cheap suit on a rainy day at Metro Airport. More than 7,000 passengers fly in and out of Metro every day. At the main McNamara terminal, Delta, security clamped down on the media so hard, we were only allowed to do interviews in the departure area. Thirty feet below, or lower level... don't even try it.

To us, that means give it a shot. We only had seconds. Fox 2 photographer Doug Tracey drove the live truck to the departure gate and dropped the cable down to the lower level where we were parked. Hooked up the cable to his truck. Had a signal. Both my second photographer, Rich Roethler, and myself jumped out of the truck... did an on-camera stand-up, which means standing, holding a microphone, and talking into the camera. Just before airport security arrived. It worked. Warning from airport security: "Don't try it again!"

With songstress and Broadway actress Stephanie Mills after interviewing her in Detroit for a promotional tour for her new album.

Morning live shot... standing in the middle of hundreds of screaming and crying teenagers in a radio station parking lot waiting for the hottest rock band in the country to arrive... the Hanson Brothers... The *who*? The *what*? Never heard of 'em. Back at the station, anchor Alan Lee knew I didn't know, asking me all types of questions, but I knew how to dance around questions... I was like a dancing machine...

Remember the Western movie, *Gunfight at the O.K. Corral*? Well, shoot-outs in certain Detroit neighborhoods could resemble the movie. Heard this all too often. Victim is shot... picked up by EMS leaving the scene... the back door of the EMS truck opens... a gunman

"We're Standing By"

begins firing at the victim, making sure he is dead. More crime drama. Another shooting, no one is talking. Detroit homicide detectives warning us, they are leaving the crime scene... we suggest you do the same... welcome to the big city...

That's me on the left, holding the microphone. I'm covered with dust while covering the implosion of the iconic Hudson's building downtown Detroit. It was so quiet, you could hear dust hitting the ground. And the dust was so thick, I couldn't see my camera man.

Chapter 8

Livernois Riot

EIGHT YEARS AFTER THE Detroit riots of 1967, another riot exploded on Detroit streets. It was the summer of 1975. The Motor City had elected its first black mayor, Coleman Young. He ran on a campaign of integrating city workers, police, fire, and civil servants. But the hot summer of 1967 continued to smolder eight years later.

Blacks, blacked out of jobs, remained on the radar of police brutality. In the summer of 1975, the social ingredient for another violent uprising spilled over on Livernois Avenue near Fenkell Avenue.

Bob Bolton's Bar, a known hangout for white Detroit's finest in a neighborhood that is mostly black. It was like a gun unlocked and loaded waiting for someone to pull the trigger. Reportedly, a young black male was attempting to steal a car in the bar's parking lot. Bar owner Bob Bolton saw what was going on. Came outside, confronted the young black male. Shots fired, the black male was killed. At the time, there was no social media, but word traveled fast. Within hours, the hot night turned into a hot mess. Armed Detroit police in front of the bar. Across the street an angry black mob began to assemble. Bricks, bottles, and bullets turned Livernois into a war zone.

Subsequently, a member of Mayor Young's security called me at home. Told me to get to Livernois ASAP. I called Burt Allen; he

"We're Standing By"

was a news reporter for CKLW, the Canadian station, right across the bridge. We met in the parking lot of Tip Town Bar B Que (great ribs).

As a reporter, you run to, not from, trouble. As a journalist, always being at the right place at the wrong time. First, interview the police. Facing an angry crowd, along with police, we were dodging bricks and bottles, even a few Molotov cocktails. To be fair, we crossed the street to interview members of the angry mob. This time we faced the police, becoming targets of tear gas, smoke bombs, and gunfire. Eyes watering, banged up and bruised, Burt had the equipment to feed sound back to the station. Me, had to find a phone booth to verbally describe what was going on.

On the air, WJLB radio personality K. B., Ken Bell, gave me the green light to cut into music programming. A first for a black music station in our area. Burt and I were reporting until about two in the morning. There were dozens of arrests and even more injuries. The riot calmed down. Several businesses were damaged or destroyed. Fortunately, the riot did not spread to other neighborhoods.

No sleep, smelled like I had not bathed in a few days, headed back to the station, writing and editing sound bites of the violence and chaos. Station Manager Norm Miller and Sales Manager Commodore Clark had nothing but praise of the riot coverage. Mixing music and information to Detroit's African American community is being compared to a happy marriage. With bigger and better things to come...

Sound Bites

Wake up... Wake up... Me and the crew, Doug Tracey, Gregg Walterhouse, slept through a 7:30 a.m. live shot. Told the show producer a lie. She believed it...

Not on TV... I was on the big screen... Played myself in the Michael Moore Oscar-winning documentary *Bowling for Columbine*, a documentary that explores gun violence.

Oops, I forgot... On the air live... Walking and talking, sometimes I would forget to step back in front of the camera. My shooter had to remind me... "Hey, Al, camera!"

"We're Standing By"

With longtime WXYZ reporter Bill Proctor (left), Anqunette "Q" Jamison, and her husband, Richard.

With Rhonda Walker (center) and Gregg Tatchio.

We had a studio built in the press room of the Coleman A. Young Municipal Center to do live shots. Here I'm with shooter Paul Kowal. I was the City Hall reporter.

With Karen Dumas (center) at her 50th birthday party and fashion editor Chuck Bennett.

Chapter 9

You Own the Story... "Breaking News"

Breaking news... This is the Holy Grail for a journalist. The bigger the breaking news story, the better. Breaking news brings you audience recognition, credibility, journalism awards, and leadership in the journalism community.

Breaking news is not showtime. It's prime time. On the streets it's not time for the pimps and players. It's time for the "Mack Daddy." Adrenaline flowing like a river. Experience is the key. Put down your pen and paper. Everything off the cuff. Delivering what you know in a calm but deliberate voice. Your heart pounding, sweating, but you can't show it.

In television, you have a team: one photographer is shooting video; the other setting up the live truck. The reporter is gathering information... Tick... Tick... the clock is ticking, the producer is yelling in your ear... Hurry up. We are close to showtime.

Depending on the time, instead of editing tape, it's fed back raw, or we roll the video from the live truck as the reporter is on the air. This is prime time. The objective? Get as much information as you can, make sure it's factual, and report it with the goal of beating the competition.

"We're Standing By"

Breaking news can drain you, but you keep going. Dead bodies, bloody scene, head blown off, brain matter splattered everywhere. I have seen it and reported it all, dozens of times, live. Breaking news. It's big and happening live and now...

Sound Bites

Hey, Al, who was that? Interviewed hundreds, maybe thousands of people over the years. Outside doing live shots, people would walk up and wanted to talk. Sometimes they would almost interrupt the live shot. They wanted to take pictures and sign autographs. Shooters Patty Larin, Mike Moore, Labe Waddell, and others would ask, "Al, who was that?" My response: "I don't know." They would laugh, "Hey, Al, hope you remember us after you retire."

Stumbling on a great story... Burt Allen and I riding down an escalator, leaving a story in the Renaissance Center, looked down and saw then-Governor Bill Milliken sitting alone on a sofa. Asked the Governor if we could do an interview. He said yes. Had exclusives on several stories...

What was I thinking about? After winning the Robert F. Kennedy journalism award, network radio job offers started pouring in. First CBS: weekend anchor during the week. Turned it down. My wife did not want to leave Detroit. Several months later, a similar offer from NBC. Again, had to turn it down. My wife did not want to leave her family.

Nothing is funny about this sound bite... When it comes to comedians. This was not a joke.

First, Bill Cosby refused to do an interview surrounding the controversial Ford Pinto. He was the pitchman when the Pinto was crashed in the rear, the gas tank exploded, causing injury to the passengers. I was persistent. Cosby leaned down and told me, "You do understand English, don't you?"

Comedian Steve Harvey brought his syndicated radio show to Detroit as part of a fundraiser for Detroit Public Schools. Harvey told us quit harassing him. He was too busy to talk on camera. That's not funny.

Sharing a laugh with shooter Patty Larin.

"We're Standing By"

Top: Me as a boy in Little Rock, Arkansas.
Below: Near Hot Springs, Arkansas, with (left to right): my mother, Doris Long; my grandmother, Big Mama; and Grandad, Ethridge Hugh McFarlin, known as "Bookie," the first black police officer in Little Rock, Arkansas.

CHAPTER 10

Right Place at the Wrong Time

Growing up, journalism was my childhood sweetheart. But I often found myself at the right place but at the wrong time. We moved around a lot. Living in public housing can be fun, funky, and fatal. An example: playing outside, witnessed several teenagers arguing, then fighting... Watch out for gun play. One teen was shot. My friends started running away. I choose to run towards the gunfire. One teenager was seriously wounded. There I was.

At that time, Little Rock was a big rock smothered in racial hatred. Public places, like bathrooms, restaurants, movie theaters, even water fountains were segregated, along with public schools. Well, the winds of change were about to explode. Then-governor of Arkansas Orval Faubus made it known that there would be no integration between niggers and whites in public schools in Arkansas following the US Supreme Court's *Brown v. Board of Education* decision, outlawing segregation in public schools in Kansas.

Well, a feisty black woman, Daisy Bates, head of the local NAACP chapter, vowed, "There is gonna be a change." In 1957, this small black woman led nine black high school students to all-white Central High School in an attempt to register the Little Rock Nine, as they were called. As expected, they were turned away.

Bates would not back down. The National Guard was called in.

"We're Standing By"

Then President Eisenhower stepped in. The US Army was brought in to keep order and open the door to allow the Little Rock Nine to register and attend Central High School.

Guess who witnessed this ugly racial mess? Yours truly. We lived across the street from Ernest Green's home. He was the oldest of the Nine. He had a younger brother, stricken with polio, a crippling disease that affected the legs, making it difficult to walk. Polio was eventually eradicated in the US. Ernest Green's mother was my fourth-grade teacher. Standing there, I was a witness to the brutal racial attacks and the name-calling perpetrated by white students and adults.

Segregation would not stop our grandfather. We called him Bookie. He became Little Rock's first black police officer, assigned to foot patrol in a rough area of the city's black community.

Bookie also voted in the 1952 presidential election at a time when blacks were banned from voting. To vote, he had to pay a five-dollar poll tax. Whites? No charge. How did I know? I was standing there.

I never will forget one bloody and violent incident. My mother and I were riding on the bus downtown — of course, we had to sit in the back. Another black couple was sitting near us. He was brown complexioned; she was light and could also pass for white. Another bus stop, three white teenagers boarded the bus. Saw the black couple, walked towards the back, began yelling at the female, calling her "nigger lover." She yelled back, "I am black!" That's when the trio began beating the black man.

My mother told me to close my eyes, but I could still see as they beat and kicked their victim. He never fought back. Outnumbered, the white teenagers assaulted him as though he was a punching bag, beating him off the bus, leaving a trail of blood. Did he survive? I never knew.

The question I always ask myself... Does the color of someone's skin make a person that violent?

CHAPTER 11

Are Television Newsrooms Black and White?

AS JOURNALISTS, OUR STORIES often cover the human tragedies, even race relations. We sometimes paint a picture of racial harmony, but as we know, decades later, nothing has really changed that much since the famed Civil Rights Movement of the 1950s and 1960s. There are only a few cracks in the glass ceiling. Poverty prevails as if time stood still.

As a people, we continue to work twice as hard as our white counterparts just to get a small piece of the American Dream. Many Northern big cities treated blacks worse in some cases than some Southern states. Housing, jobs, education, and promotions — just a dream. There's an old saying in the black community, "What you see is what you get." Nothing.

In the so-called liberal news media, what you see in front of the camera is not what you get behind the camera. African Americans still have a long road to travel when it comes to editorial decision-making. The National Association of Black Journalists and other civil rights organizations have been waging a fierce battle to make newsrooms inclusive, not only by placing African Americans in front of the camera, but also behind the scenes in management positions, such as general managers, news directors, and executive producers. In the 1980, we formed the local chapter of NABJ in Detroit.

In Detroit, we've had debates, discussions, and discord when it came to hiring not only talent, but behind-the-scenes decision makers. The old excuse "cannot find a qualified person" is out. Who is fooling who?

Management change? You could hear us publicly complain: *Where are the blacks, male or female*? African Americans in the Fox 2 newsroom created a united front asking for change. Not much changed over the years. As journalists, we are supposed to give the people a voice, but which voice are you talking about?

During my tour of duty, Channel 4 only had one black news director, Bob Warfield; Channel 7, one black news director; and Fox 2, none. There's one human resource director. We have not given up the fight…

Sound Bites

Covering the Mayor Coleman Young deathwatch at Sinai Hospital… My mother lived across the street. Saw all the live trucks lined up. She came out, went to my live truck, asked me had I eaten breakfast. I told her no. She went home, prepared breakfast for not only me, but the nearly 10 other people who were covering Coleman Young. The menu: all homemade, ham and cheese omelets, hash browns, and English muffins. My two sisters, Donna and Beverly, brought the food over, complete with plasticware, salt and pepper, and napkins. This was not a one-day assignment. Mama kept everyone full.

My mother could sometimes be my worst critic. She would call the station, and say, "Tell that boy to put on a hat," or "He's standing too close to the street!"

Are Television Newsrooms Black and White?

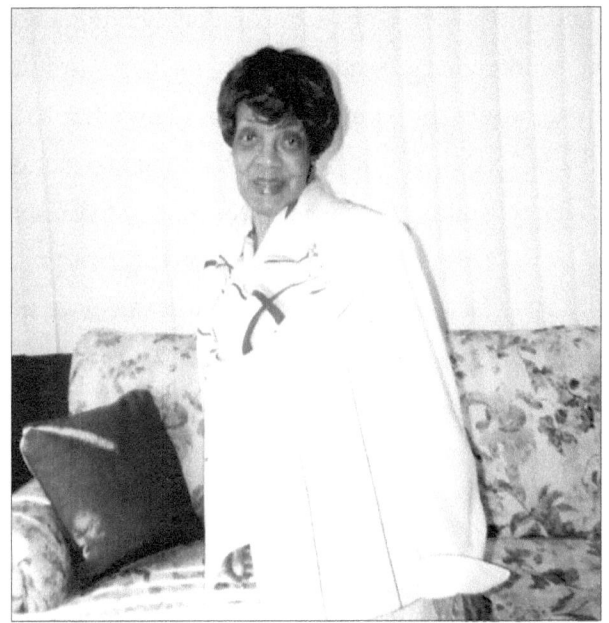

My mother, my biggest fan.

With my two sisters: Beverly on the left, Donna on the right, and Beverly's children, Craig and Pam.

"We're Standing By"

It was an honor... Covering the funeral of civil rights activist Rosa Parks from Montgomery, Alabama. This included traveling to the nation's capital, where she would lie in state, then return to Detroit for funeral services. In DC, thousands lined the funeral procession. I told my photographer, Rodney Ferguson, that I wanted to do a stand-up in front of the crowd. Did the stand-up and to my surprise, the people lining the route gave me a huge cheer. I still don't remember what I said.

Covering a Nazi rally on the steps of the Dearborn City Hall. It was Bob Bennett from Channel 4, Bill Proctor from Channel 7, Bill Black from WJR Radio, and me. All black reporters. The head of the Nazi rally spewing racial hatred aimed at Jews and blacks. He looked down at us and said, "Not talking about you guys."

Chapter 12

Never Kiss and Tell

JOURNALISM HAS A LOT of rules, and one of the most important ones is, "Never kiss and tell." That means protect your sources — the people who secretly give you information — at all times, no matter what. Without the inside scoop, you have no story.

What is a journalist? They are messengers, repeating what someone told them on the air or in print. Is it the truth, revenge, or jealousy? That's the reporter's job: fitting the pieces of the puzzle together. The number-one rule: check with three sources. If they are all saying the same thing, then you can run with the information.

Sources are your bread and butter. The missing link to a chain of "he said, she said" determines fact over fiction. Be careful: this is the information that can cost someone a job, a career, even send someone to prison. It's like walking on eggs while wearing cleats.

Developing a source is like cultivating a garden. Planting seeds... It takes time to grow. I think the main reason I was hired at Channel 2 was because of the sources I could contact with just one phone call.

Most importantly, never reveal your sources, and even risk going to jail to protect them. My colleague Bill Gallagher and I fiercely believed in protecting sources at all costs. We even went so far as to store a change of clothes and hygiene products in our lockers. Case in point, one of our producers was sent to the Wayne County jail, after refusing to name his source in a high-profile criminal case. The producer spent a couple of days behind bars before being released. He never told authorities the names of his contact related to the case. Most sources are not looking for money or fame. They're just about doing the right thing when they see something that is not right.

One of my best sources — can't reveal her name, just call her K.J. — was well-connected with the movers and shakers, from the governor's office to the street sweeper and all those in between. Because of her position, she was a trusted confidant. She knew where the dirt was, and who was dirty. Sources come in all shapes and sizes, male or female, politicians and preachers. They can make your day.

While working at WJLB, I received a phone call from a Wayne County sheriff's deputy. "Hey, Al, we got a superstar entertainer locked up in the Wayne County jail. Get down here. He may talk to you."

To my surprise, it was Eddie Kendricks, a member of the Temptations. Locked up for back child support. Yes, he did talk, and I had an exclusive jailhouse interview. Another example: three people shot to death, execution-style in an abandoned house. Reported the story on the air. A few hours later, got a strange phone call. Person on the line would not give his name, but told me he heard I could be trusted.

His information: "I will give you a license plate number. It's connected to the triple homicide." Sure enough, the license plate number I gave to police led to the arrest of several people involved in the triple homicide. Detroit police homicide detectives told me it was all drug related, and where did I get my information from...

Over the years, the number of credible sources has grown, but there is one drawback. There are some great high-profile stories I can never reveal...

Footnote: One story I missed, and it was huge. For weeks, heard rumors about a downtown law firm cheating clients out of their settlements. Either I was asleep at the wheel or just not paying attention. The Ed Bell Law Firm was right across the street from WJLB. Then it exploded. A man walks into the Ed Bell Law Firm in the Buhl Building. Armed with two Molotov cocktails and a shotgun. Opens fire, killing the secretary, wounding one of Bell's law partners, before the gunman was apprehended. Attorney Bell was not even in the office...

CHAPTER 13

So, You Want to Be a Journalist?

So, you have a smartphone, notepad, and pen, and you look good, dressed for success. You tell family and friends being a journalist is cool, and it will make you famous.

Your dream is about to turn into a nightmare. Here is the real deal. You believe everything you hear, and you don't bother to check your true sources because you don't have any. If you did, would you be willing to go to jail to protect your source?

Journalists work long hours, including holidays and weekends. Have any kids? You will miss games and other family events. Get calls in the middle of the night to cover a breaking story, and with very little experience, your first job may be in "Hot Town" Mississippi, or some other tiny town, making low wages.

Broadcast news can be a fickle profession. In everyone's contract, there's one sentence that stands out: "You can be fired for just cause." Meaning, if your tie is crooked, goodbye.

There are exceptions, Rhonda Walker came to Channel 2 with very little experience. She did traffic; she was terrific. Went on to anchor at WDIV, Channel 4. Teachers and instructors at colleges and universities teach theory, but hands-on is the best experience. That's why internships are so important.

One of my biggest complaints: journalism should be taught by journalists. On many campuses, some teachers have never been inside a newsroom. Educators are taught by educators. Medical residents are taught by doctors. When it comes to writing in television news, you write to video. And sentences are often declarative statements. For instance, "The apartment building was destroyed by fire. Dozens of residents have to find another place to live."

Asking questions? Know the answer *before* you ask the question. You will be surprised at the response. Also, take a foreign language. It will help you pronounce words. If you stumble doing a live shot, don't stop to apologize; the audience will never know.

There were two things I did almost every day before going to work: had a hot cup of tea with a slice of fresh lemon when the tea kettle whistles. And I would say a short prayer, because I know it's going to be a hell of a day. By the way, drinking hot tea every day… never lost my voice or had a sore throat.

Chapter 14

Who is Al Allen?

SOMETIMES, GRANDMA KNOWS BEST. She told my mother, "That boy is going to be a lawyer or politician because he lies a lot."

Well, instead I became a journalist, and I don't lie a lot (smile). Instead of Al Allen, my real name is Andrew Long. My second job in radio... The program director could not stand Andrew Long. Said it was too hard to pronounce, plus listeners would not remember the name... (Really?) I just picked a name: Al Allen. I must have seen it somewhere. Back in the day, unless you had a common name, on-air talent would use an alias, radio and television. Today, you can use your real name.

I love being a spectator to news events. In many cases, history-making events. Talking and listening to people at their most vulnerable moments. We see the good and the bad. As the Fifth Estate, we are protected by the First Amendment to the Constitution, but in my mind, journalism is not a right, but a privilege, not to be abused.

My work ethic is the blue-collar approach: always in the trenches, working extremely hard, never accepting defeat. As an African American, I was taught to work three times as hard because of racism in America. The same lesson was passed on to our son.

Being a journalist, I can keep a secret; that's how you accumulate and establish trust with sources. I never took my work home, but working long hours, sometimes six or seven days a week, cultivating and maintaining sources, other outside projects like speaking engagements and the music business began to have a negative impact on our marriage. There were some bumps and detours. Alfreda and I put our heads together and worked it out.

With Alfreda, my wife of 51 years.

However, years earlier, back in 1968, Alfreda's health problems took center stage. Andrew Junior was born in June of 1968. Healthy... 10 fingers and 10 toes. But Alfreda developed a bowel obstruction, which is a serious digestive problem involving the intestines. She was born with it and had had emergency surgery when she was just hours old. When our son was born, that bowel obstruction came back as a bowel *destruction*. During the emergency surgery, we almost lost Alfreda twice. Spent two months in the hospital. Her two great aunts and myself shared babysitting duties taking care of Andrew Jr. Finally, Alfreda was able to come home.

Our son, Andrew Jr. and his wife, Yolanda, and with me, before we head to The Roostertail where I received an award in 2013.

Over the years, Alfreda had a number of health issues. Around the mid-1990s, Alfreda's health was hit with another curve ball. A freak accident... She fell and broke her leg. Everything went south.

1. That bowel obstruction erupted again. Three major surgeries at the University of Michigan Hospital. The surgeries were not successful.

2. Next, her kidneys failed.

3. Then the bombshell — the big "C" — cancer, multi myeloma, a form of bone cancer.

4. There is no cure.

Me? I would have checked out a long time ago.

Alfreda is as tough as nails. Deeply religious, loves life, her church, St. Andrew A.M.E., says lots of prayers, adores our two grandsons, Andrew and Evan. Continues to make the best out of a bad situation. Strongly believes it's GOD that keeps her alive.

Alfreda's continued health problems weigh heavily on our son

Andrew Jr. and his family — wife, Yolanda, and grandsons, Andrew III and Evan Nicholas. We're in Detroit. They're about 2,000 miles away in Seattle, Washington. We visit Seattle often, take vacations together… Nothing like being together in one city; however, we continue to be a long-distance family, and have found a way to "work it out," in the lyrics of a popular Gospel song…

As a journalist, you often can carry a major liability, pessimism or doubt, because you are often fed a steady diet of lies, hidden agendas, corruption, criminals, and high-profile people living double lives. At the end of the day, there is optimism and hope.

My achievements are the result of others opening the door. That means you have to reach down and help others to achieve or you are not doing your job. Examples of the many ambitious young journalists I've helped include former interns who are making a difference:

- Pam Moore, anchor queen in San Francisco;

- Kevin Harry, executive producer of *Inside Edition*; and

- Kennan Oliphant, TV news director in Cincinnati, Ohio.

If you are a successful African American, it is your responsibility — even duty — to open the door for other African Americans.

So how did my first radio job happen? By accident, being at the right place and the right time for a change. Second year college student at Arkansas A&M in Pine Bluff, majoring in business and communication. Driving — made a wrong turn and stumbled on radio station KCAT. Went in, explained to the secretary that I was a college student, majoring in communication, looking for a job. Didn't even fill out an application. The program director liked my voice. I did everything from DJ, news, sales, even mopped the floor. I was multi-tasking before multi-tasking became a thing. All this, while still in school.

Who is Al Allen?

Job number two. For me this was a giant step. Landed a job at KOKY-AM in Little Rock. Disc jockey and news anchor. Worked with the legendary "Jocko" Smith. He was the air personality who described soul music as "dirty, filthy and nasty music."

KOKY was where I had to change my name; the program director did not like Andrew Long. He said it was too hard to pronounce and listeners would not remember the name. It had to be catchy. So Andrew Long became Al Allen, just off the top of my head. Still in school, also working on the air, I had enough hours to graduate, but never walked across the stage.

I racked up a lot of miles driving back and forth from Detroit to Little Rock. I had a wife and child back in the Motor City. So, it was time for me to find a job close to home. Fortunate enough, I started working for WGPR-FM as a news anchor/board operator...

I always loved to compete. Winning is in my DNA, along with working in radio and television. I always dreamed of becoming a network correspondent. I was a big fan of *60 Minutes*, especially the late Ed Bradley. Network correspondent? Never applied. What kept my head on my shoulders and eyes on the prize? A program director told me, "You are only as good as your last newscast, and your last newscast was not that good."

Chapter 15

Is it Real or Fake News?

BACK IN THE DAY, what happened between the sheets stayed between the sheets. As legitimate journalists, we believed that sultry, sensational, and raunchy stories involving high-profile politicians, corporate executives, athletes, and so on… were nobody's business, except their own. Rumors about gays and lesbians stayed in the closet.

Now if you were found corrupt, criminal, or abusing taxpayer dollars, then it was hands on. After all, the old idiom, "Loose lips sink ships," could destroy careers, credibility, even lead to prison time. So we had to be extremely careful.

Today, because of social media, we are dealing with jackleg journalists. ("Jackleg" is a Southern term for unskilled or incompetent.) Checking with reliable sources, making sure what you heard is absolutely correct… These journalistic rules are just words on paper. Now you have these blogs and podcasts being used as a platform to create just about anything. That includes between-the-sheets stories. The words "allege" or "sources said" can be used as a security blanket to cover up fake news.

There is so much information or misinformation, many times you can't check it out. And sometimes, so-called sources give you information that may be blatant lies, hoping you will be deceived into pushing their hidden agenda by broadcasting their bogus news. Truthfully, jealousy and revenge are taking over legitimate and legal news stories. If it sounds too good to be true, then it probably is. Our mission is to provide the voice of the voiceless… hope for the hopeless.

Chapter 16

Colder than a Well Digger's Ass in Montana

What is it that viewers and listeners remember most about Al Allen?

I get more questions about this than anything else…

Not the nearly half-century as a broadcast journalist.

All of the journalism awards.

All the exclusive stories.

All the sources.

All the documentaries and special reports.

No, it's the weather-related live shots and stories. Heavy rains and hurricane-force winds, blowing my umbrella away during live shots.

But the worst, standing on a freeway overpass during blizzards and bitter cold conditions. Snow so heavy it's blowing sideways, striking your face like a box cutter, turning you into a snowman in a matter of minutes.

You saw me in front of the camera, but there were two other people behind the camera. One operating the live truck, the other operating the camera. We were knee-deep in snow. The wind howling, temperature five to ten degrees below zero, feels like 20 below. Eyes tearing, lips almost frozen… hard to form words. Snot running down your nose… Thank goodness for handkerchiefs. You could only put on several layers of clothes, making it difficult to walk. Cold to the bone… Colder than a well digger's ass in Montana.

One major rule before a live shot… You must be in front of the camera two minutes before the live shot starts. Audio and video, everything has to be checked out before the live hit. But in the bitter cold and wind, with the temp around five below, the Al Allen Rule took effect: I was only in front of the camera 30 seconds before a live shot. Producers would hit the ceiling. But, it would work because everything was checked out in the truck. Just plug in when we get outside. Pray everything worked.

One morning, preparing for a live shot… Very cold, about 20 degrees. Weatherman Ben Bailey predicting partly cloudy skies, cold, but no snow in the Metro area, tossed to my live shot turning into a big snowflake. Told Ben live, hope you are not getting paid for this weather forecast.

How did we pick freeway overpasses during snowstorms? Well, my shooters actually checked out freeway overpasses during warmer weather. Critical, because distance and location can interfere with the control room getting a signal. If it worked, get ready for winter.

My decision to cover bad weather was nothing but marketing. Viewers would tell me they felt sorry for this old man standing outside in brutal, cold weather, but they would watch just to see. This attracted more viewers. It was a little show business tossed in, but it worked. Damn, it was cold!

Sound Bites

Al Allen takes on show producer...

War of words turns into a battle of fists. Did a live shot hanging from a zipline in a sporting goods store. The live shot was a disaster. Came back to the station to explain what happened. Confronted by show producer Glenn Therrien. Pointed his finger in my face. Called me a pip-squeak. I called him with my fist. We were rolling on the floor. News Director Mort Meisner broke it up. We both apologized. Friends ever since.

Fists were flying as the music was playing. Never expected this. My news anchor Greg Anthony was in the main studio talking with Larry "Doc" Elliot. Well, the conversation turned into a major brawl. I saw what was going on, grabbed production manager John Tatum. We went into the studio and broke up the brouhaha. Management never knew what happened.

Another sour note at WJLB: a female on-air personality missed her afternoon slot, late for work. When she did arrive, her hair was all over her head. White powder around her mouth and nose (cocaine), smelled like she was busy in bed. Female staff cleaned her up. She went on the air as if nothing ever happened.

Caught off guard. Sent to do a story with the Queen of Soul, Aretha Franklin. As we were walking into the Music Hall, Miss Franklin was doing a mike check. She saw me, stopped, and said, "Hello, Mr. Allen," caught me off guard, all I could say was, "Hello, Miss Queen."

Chapter 17

Open the Door – Let Me In

THERE ARE THOUSANDS OF broadcast and print journalists. Each may have a story to tell. At the urging of close friends and colleagues, I decided to tell my own story. Don't remember me, but remember what I said. Well, turned out to be just the opposite. Breaking into this crazy profession was as hard as a brick. Born in the South, I was told:

1. Your Southern accent needs to be changed.

2. You have a face for radio.

3. You don't have enough experience for major market.

4. Choose another profession.

Well, after nearly 50 years, I silenced the doubters. However, at times I doubted myself, even made some mistakes.

Growing up in the segregated South, one lesson you learned: the drumbeat to success depends on you. You have to be at least three times as smart as they (white folks) are because many believe you are destined to fail. Last hired, first fired. Don't complain. Let your work speak for your qualifications.

Former WJLB music director, the late Al Perkins, told me: let your name be the foundation on which you build your success. My success was not about me; instead, it was a team of others opening doors and giving advice.

More times than not, we are often described as the whipping boy of bad news, and that's because of the number of bad people who risk their careers for the sake of a few dollars. It's people like that who keep us employed. There's an old saying, "Power corrupts." They start out being saints and end up becoming sinners.

Being an African American, you have a responsibility to make sure the door remains open to reach out and help other African Americans to achieve similar success. If not, you have failed.

Being a responsible journalist, you have an obligation to:

1. Inform

2. Educate

3. Inspire

4. Entertain.

Open the Door. Let Me In.

I was the breaking news this day, announcing my retirement.
My son and grandsons joined me and Fox 2 News Morning Anchor
Jason Carr during a special segment to celebrate my retirement.
Photo: Mike Moore. Photograph courtesy of station WJBK.

CHAPTER 18

Bad News in the Big City

THE SMELL OF DEAD bodies choking a city. Blood flowing on the streets like hot lava from a volcano. Drugs are king, homicides just a misdemeanor. Today the word "dope" means "great." Back in the 1970s, dope meant death. Detroit's African American community assaulted by a vicious cycle of drug-related murders. In 1973 alone, nearly 700. The FBI labeling the Motor City the murder capital.

Drug dealers paying children as young as nine years old to sell ("sling") drugs on the mean streets. At that time, prosecutors say they could not prosecute the children because of their age.

How about two young boys outside playing football on a Sunday in December 1973? This game turned violent, then deadly. Eight-year-old Gerald Craft and six-year-old Keith Arnold. The boys kidnapped, held for a $50,000 ransom.

Anchoring at WJLB, the city's narcotics squad telling us that the Arnold boy was the target of the kidnapping. His relatives were involved in a drug feud. The Craft boy just happened to be at the wrong place at the wrong time. Tipsters in the police narcotics unit called me several hours after the kidnapping, confirming there was a kidnapping and ransom demand. Telling us this was a vicious crime centered around revenge and drugs. The Arnold family telling police they were innocent. Then the race to find the kidnappers. My tipsters telling me they were looking for three 21-year-old males. We showed up at three different locations over a three-day period.

Finally, one tipster told me the tragic news. The boys had been found dead in a ditch near Metro Airport. Bound, gagged, on their knees. Both shot to death execution style. The ransom never paid. A few days later the kidnappers apprehended. The trio found guilty. The verdict: prison for life.

People would always ask me what stories do you remember the most... This one at the top of the list. Outrage and outcry, senseless and ruthless from the residents. History has a habit of repeating itself. Nearly 50 years, drugs still have a clamp on the community... Spreading to the suburbs... children... caught up and killed.

So many black families came to Detroit to escape poverty and racism in the South, hoping for a better life here. Didn't find it.

Instead, more bad news in the big city.

Fifty years later, what's on the menu? Drugs smothering a nation from city to suburbs. When it comes to children, it's a buffet of violence. Children. Victims of drive-bys. Children. Slaughtered victims of school rampages.

For dessert? It's not sweet. Leaving a sour taste. As professional journalists, we deliver the message.

We're Standing By...

"We're Standing By"

Photograph courtesy of station WJBK.

This photo was taken by Bill Eisner, the unofficial photographer for the Detroit Fire Department and Detroit Police Department. Bill wrote the caption.

Over my 50-year career in broadcast news, I have covered fires, blizzards, crimes, politics, trials, funerals, you name it! I always had a legal pad in hand to write my stories. However, most of my live reports were ad libbed. Sometimes it was cold, smoky, hectic, and scary. But boy, was it fun!

Biography

AFTER A HALF-CENTURY CAREER in journalism, Al Allen is known and loved as a legend and an icon by viewers across Southeastern Michigan.

Born Andrew Long in segregated Little Rock, Arkansas, he moved to Detroit with his family as a teenager, and attended Mumford High School. There he fell in love with journalism while reporting on trends and events for the school's internal news broadcast, *Spotlight on Mumford*.

He returned to Little Rock in 1969 to serve as news director at KOKY radio. Two years later, he moved back to Detroit, becoming a reporter and news director at WCXI-AM and WGPR-FM, then as news and public affairs director at WJLB-FM. Al began his 28-year career with WJBK Fox 2 News in March of 1984.

Al's commitment to high-integrity journalism earned him many local and national awards. United Press International and the Associated Press both awarded him for his reporting on *"The Otto Wendell Story."* UPI and AP, along with the National Association of Black Journalists, bestowed Al with awards for *"Merry-Go-Round of Denial: The Black Alcoholic."* His trailblazing work on *"Crime by Color, Black on Black,"* a documentary that examined the issues surrounding black-on-black crime in Detroit, earned him The Robert F. Kennedy

Awards for Excellence in Journalism. And his report — *"Motown: Where Did Our Love Go?"* — earned an Associated Press award and was nominated for an Emmy from the National Academy of Television Arts and Sciences.

Al retired from Fox 2 News in 2012.

He celebrates 51 years of marriage to Alfreda Long, and enjoys spending time with his son, Andrew Long, Jr.; daughter-in-law, Yolanda; and his two grandsons, Andrew III and Evan.

www.ingramcontent.com/pod-product-compliance
Lightning Source LLC
Chambersburg PA
CBHW021157080526
44588CB00008B/386